THE SOUND
AND THE FURY

William Faulkner

TECHNICAL DIRECTOR Maxwell Krohn
EDITORIAL DIRECTOR Justin Kestler
MANAGING EDITOR Ben Florman

SERIES EDITORS Boomie Aglietti, Justin Kestler
PRODUCTION Christian Lorentzen

WRITERS Brian Phillips, Evan Johnson
EDITORS Matt Blanchard, Justin Kestler

This edition published by Spark Publishing

Spark Publishing
A Division of SparkNotes LLC
120 Fifth Avenue, 8th Floor
New York, NY 10011

02 03 04 05 SN 9 8 7 6 5 4 3 2 1

Please send all comments and questions or report errors to
feedback@sparknotes.com.

Library of Congress information available upon request

Printed and bound in the United States

RRD-C

ISBN 1-58663-436-4

INTRODUCTION: STOPPING TO BUY SPARKNOTES ON A SNOWY EVENING

Whose words these are you *think* you know.
Your paper's due tomorrow, though;
We're glad to see you stopping here
To get some help before you go.

Lost your course? You'll find it here.
Face tests and essays without fear.
Between the words, good grades at stake:
Get great results throughout the year.

Once school bells caused your heart to quake
As teachers circled each mistake.
Use SparkNotes and no longer weep,
Ace every single test you take.

Yes, books are lovely, dark, and deep,
But only what you grasp you keep,
With hours to go before you sleep,
With hours to go before you sleep.

Contents

CONTEXT

WILLIAM FAULKNER WAS BORN in 1897 in New Albany, Mississippi, to a prominent Southern family. A number of his ancestors were involved in the Mexican-American War, the Civil War, and the Reconstruction, and were part of the local railroad industry and political scene. Faulkner showed signs of artistic talent from a young age, but became bored with his classes and never finished high school.

Faulkner grew up in the town of Oxford, Mississippi, and eventually returned there in his later years and purchased his famous estate, Rowan Oak. Oxford and the surrounding area were Faulkner's inspiration for the fictional Yoknapatawpha County, Mississippi, and its town of Jefferson. These locales became the setting for a number of his works. Faulkner's "Yoknapatawpha novels" include *The Sound and the Fury* (1929), *As I Lay Dying* (1930), *Light in August* (1932), *Absalom, Absalom!* (1936), *The Hamlet* (1940), and *Go Down, Moses* (1942), and they feature some of the same characters and locations.

Faulkner was particularly interested in the decline of the Deep South after the Civil War. Many of his novels explore the deterioration of the Southern aristocracy after the destruction of its wealth and way of life during the Civil War and Reconstruction. Faulkner populates Yoknapatawpha County with the skeletons of old mansions and the ghosts of great men, patriarchs and generals from the past whose aristocratic families fail to live up to their historical greatness. Beneath the shadow of past grandeur, these families attempt to cling to old Southern values, codes, and myths that are corrupted and out of place in the reality of the modern world. The families in Faulkner's novels are rife with failed sons, disgraced daughters, and smoldering resentments between whites and blacks in the aftermath of African-American slavery.

Faulkner's reputation as one of the greatest novelists of the twentieth century is largely due to his highly experimental style. Faulkner was a pioneer in literary modernism, dramatically diverging from the forms and structures traditionally used in novels before his time. Faulkner often employs stream of consciousness narrative, discards any notion of chronological order, uses multiple narrators, shifts

CONTEXT

between the present and past tense, and tends toward impossibly long and complex sentences. Not surprisingly, these stylistic innovations make some of Faulkner's novels incredibly challenging to the reader. However, these bold innovations paved the way for countless future writers to continue to experiment with the possibilities of the English language. For his efforts, Faulkner was awarded the Nobel Prize in Literature in 1949. He died in Mississippi in 1962.

First published in 1929, *The Sound and the Fury* is recognized as one of the most successfully innovative and experimental American novels of its time, not to mention one of the most challenging to interpret. The novel concerns the downfall of the Compsons, who have been a prominent family in Jefferson, Mississippi, since before the Civil War. Faulkner represents the human experience by portraying events and images subjectively, through several different characters' respective memories of childhood. The novel's stream of consciousness style is frequently very opaque, as events are often deliberately obscured and narrated out of order. Despite its formidable complexity, *The Sound and the Fury* is an overpowering and deeply moving novel. It is generally regarded as Faulkner's most important and remarkable literary work.

PLOT OVERVIEW

A TTEMPTING TO APPLY traditional plot summary to *The Sound and the Fury* is difficult. At a basic level, the novel is about the three Compson brothers' obsessions with the their sister Caddy, but this brief synopsis represents merely the surface of what the novel contains. A story told in four chapters, by four different voices, and out of chronological order, *The Sound and the Fury* requires intense concentration and patience to interpret and understand.

The first three chapters of the novel consist of the convoluted thoughts, voices, and memories of the three Compson brothers, captured on three different days. The brothers are Benjy, a severely retarded thirty-three-year-old man, speaking in April, 1928; Quentin, a young Harvard student, speaking in June, 1910; and Jason, a bitter farm-supply store worker, speaking again in April, 1928. Faulkner tells the fourth chapter in his own narrative voice, but focuses on Dilsey, the Compson family's devoted "Negro" cook who has played a great part in raising the children. Faulkner harnesses the brothers' memories of their sister Caddy, using a single symbolic moment to forecast the decline of the once prominent Compson family and to examine the deterioration of the Southern aristocratic class since the Civil War.

The Compsons are one of several prominent names in the town of Jefferson, Mississippi. Their ancestors helped settle the area and subsequently defended it during the Civil War. Since the war, the Compsons have gradually seen their wealth, land, and status crumble away. Mr. Compson is an alcoholic. Mrs. Compson is a self-absorbed hypochondriac who depends almost entirely upon Dilsey to raise her four children. Quentin, the oldest child, is a sensitive bundle of neuroses. Caddy is stubborn, but loving and compassionate. Jason has been difficult and mean-spirited since birth and is largely spurned by the other children. Benjy is severely mentally disabled, an "idiot" with no understanding of the concepts of time or morality. In the absence of the self-absorbed Mrs. Compson, Caddy serves as a mother figure and symbol of affection for Benjy and Quentin.

As the children grow older, however, Caddy begins to behave promiscuously, which torments Quentin and sends Benjy into fits of moaning and crying. Quentin is preparing to go to Harvard, and

Mr. Compson sells a large portion of the family land to provide funds for the tuition. Caddy loses her virginity and becomes pregnant. She is unable or unwilling to name the father of the child, though it is likely Dalton Ames, a boy from town.

Caddy's pregnancy leaves Quentin emotionally shattered. He attempts to claim false responsibility for the pregnancy, lying to his father that he and Caddy have committed incest. Mr. Compson is indifferent to Caddy's promiscuity, dismissing Quentin's story and telling his son to leave early for the Northeast.

Attempting to cover up her indiscretions, Caddy quickly marries Herbert Head, a banker she met in Indiana. Herbert promises Jason Compson a job in his bank. Herbert immediately divorces Caddy and rescinds Jason's job offer when he realizes his wife is pregnant with another man's child. Meanwhile, Quentin, still mired in despair over Caddy's sin, commits suicide by drowning himself in the Charles River just before the end of his first year at Harvard.

The Compsons disown Caddy from the family, but take in her newborn daughter, Miss Quentin. The task of raising Miss Quentin falls squarely on Dilsey's shoulders. Mr. Compson dies of alcoholism roughly a year after Quentin's suicide. As the oldest surviving son, Jason becomes the head of the Compson household. Bitterly employed at a menial job in the local farm-supply store, Jason devises an ingenious scheme to steal the money Caddy sends to support Miss Quentin's upbringing.

Miss Quentin grows up to be an unhappy, rebellious, and promiscuous girl, constantly in conflict with her overbearing and vicious uncle Jason. On Easter Sunday, 1928, Miss Quentin steals several thousand dollars from Jason and runs away with a man from a traveling show. While Jason chases after Miss Quentin to no avail, Dilsey takes Benjy and the rest of her family to Easter services at the local church.

A NOTE ON THE TITLE

The title of *The Sound and the Fury* refers to a line from William Shakespeare's *Macbeth*. Macbeth, a Scottish general and nobleman, learns of his wife's suicide and feels that his life is crumbling into chaos. In addition to Faulkner's title, we can find several of the novel's important motifs in Macbeth's short soliloquy in Act V, scene v:

> Tomorrow, and tomorrow, and tomorrow
> Creeps in this petty pace from day to day
> To the last syllable of recorded time,
> And all our yesterdays have lighted fools
> The way to dusty death. Out, out, brief candle.
> Life's but a walking shadow, a poor player
> That struts and frets his hour upon the stage,
> And then is heard no more. It is a tale
> Told by an idiot, full of sound and fury,
> Signifying nothing.   (V.v.18–27)

The Sound and the Fury literally begins as a "tale / Told by an idiot," as the first chapter is narrated by the mentally disabled Benjy. The novel's central concerns include time, much like Macbeth's "[t]omorrow, and tomorrow"; death, recalling Macbeth's "dusty death"; and nothingness and disintegration, a clear reference to Macbeth's lament that life "[s]ignif[ies] nothing." Additionally, Quentin is haunted by the sense that the Compson family has disintegrated to a mere shadow of its former greatness.

In his soliloquy, Macbeth implies that life is but a shadow of the past and that a modern man, like himself, is inadequately equipped and unable to achieve anything near the greatness of the past. Faulkner reinterprets this idea, implying that if man does not choose to take his own life, as Quentin does, the only alternatives are to become either a cynic and materialist like Jason, or an idiot like Benjy, unable to see life as anything more than a meaningless series of images, sounds, and memories.

Character List

Jason Compson III The head of the Compson household until his death from alcoholism in 1912. Mr. Compson is the father of Quentin, Caddy, Jason IV, and Benjy, and the husband of Caroline.

Caroline Compson The self-pitying and self-absorbed wife of Mr. Compson and mother of the four Compson children. Caroline's hypochondria preoccupies her and contributes to her inability to care properly for her children.

Quentin Compson The oldest of the Compson children and the narrator of the novel's second chapter. A sensitive and intelligent boy, Quentin is preoccupied with his love for his sister Caddy and his notion of the Compson family's honor. He commits suicide by drowning himself just before the end of his first year at Harvard.

Caddy Compson The second oldest of the Compson children and the only daughter. Actually named Candace, Caddy is very close to her brother Quentin. She becomes promiscuous, gets pregnant out of wedlock, and eventually marries and divorces Herbert Head in 1910.

Jason Compson IV The second youngest of the Compson children and the narrator of the novel's third chapter. Jason is mean-spirited, petty, and very cynical.

Benjy Compson The youngest of the Compson children and narrator of the novel's first chapter. Born Maury Compson, his name is changed to Benjamin in 1900, when he is discovered to be severely mentally retarded.

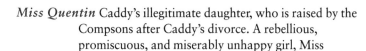

Miss Quentin Caddy's illegitimate daughter, who is raised by the Compsons after Caddy's divorce. A rebellious, promiscuous, and miserably unhappy girl, Miss Quentin eventually steals money from Jason and leaves town with a member of a traveling minstrel show.

Dilsey   The Compsons' "Negro" cook, Dilsey is a pious, strong-willed, protective woman who serves as a stabilizing force for the Compson family.

Roskus   Dilsey's husband and the Compsons' servant. Roskus suffers from a severe case of rheumatism that eventually kills him.

T.P.   One of Dilsey's sons, T.P. gets drunk with Benjy and fights with Quentin at Caddy's wedding.

Versh   Another of Dilsey's sons and Benjy's keepers.

Frony   Dilsey's daughter. Frony is also Luster's mother and works in the Compsons' kitchen.

Luster   Frony's son and Dilsey's grandson. Luster is a young boy who looks after and entertains Benjy in 1928, despite the fact that he is only half Benjy's age.

The man with the red tie The mysterious man with whom Miss Quentin allegedly elopes.

Damuddy The Compson children's grandmother, who dies when they are young.

Uncle Maury Bascomb Mrs. Compson's brother, who lives off his brother-in-law's money. Benjy is initially named after Uncle Maury, but Benjy's condition and Caroline's insecurity about her family name convince her to change her son's name.

Mr. and Mrs. Patterson The Compsons' next-door neighbors. Uncle Maury has an affair with Mrs. Patterson until Mr. Patterson intercepts a note Maury has sent to her.

Charlie One of Caddy's first suitors, whom Benjy catches with Caddy on the swing during the first chapter.

Dalton Ames A local Jefferson boy who is probably the father of Caddy's child, Miss Quentin.

Shreve MacKenzie Quentin's roommate at Harvard. A young Canadian man, Shreve reappears in *Absalom, Absalom!,* one of Faulkner's later novels, which is largely narrated by Shreve and Quentin from their dorm room at Harvard.

Spoade A Harvard senior from South Carolina. Spoade once mocked Quentin's virginity by calling Shreve Quentin's "husband."

Gerald Bland A swaggering student at Harvard. Quentin fights with Gerald because he reminds him of Dalton Ames.

Mrs. Bland Gerald Bland's boastful, Southern mother.

Deacon A black man in Cambridge, Massachusetts, to whom Quentin gives his suicide notes.

Julio The brother of an Italian girl who attaches herself to Quentin as he wanders Cambridge before his suicide.

Sydney Herbert Head The prosperous banker whom Caddy marries. Herbert later divorces Caddy because of her pregnancy.

Lorraine Jason's mistress, a prostitute who lives in Memphis.

Earl The owner of the farm-supply store where Jason works. Earl feels some loyalty toward Mrs. Compson and thus puts up with Jason's surliness.

Uncle Job A black man who works with Jason at Earl's store.

Reverend Shegog The pastor who delivers a powerful sermon on Easter Sunday at the local black church in Jefferson.

ANALYSIS OF MAJOR CHARACTERS

MR. JASON COMPSON III

Mr. Compson is a well-spoken but very cynical and detached man. He subscribes to a philosophy of determinism and fatalism—he believes life is essentially meaningless and that he can do little to change the events that befall his family. Despite his cynicism, however, Mr. Compson maintains notions of gentlemanliness and family honor, which Quentin inherits. Mr. Compson risks the family's financial well-being in exchange for the potential prestige of Quentin's Harvard education, and he tells stories that foster Quentin's nearly fanatical obsession with the family name.

Though he inculcates his son with the concept of family honor, Mr. Compson is unconcerned with it in practice. He acts indifferent to Quentin about Caddy's pregnancy, telling him to accept it as a natural womanly shortcoming. Mr. Compson's indifference greatly upsets Quentin, who is ashamed by his father's disregard for traditional Southern ideals of honor and virtue. Mr. Compson dismisses Quentin's concerns about Caddy and tells his son not to take himself so seriously, which initiates Quentin's rapid fall toward depression and suicide. Mr. Compson dies of alcoholism shortly thereafter.

MRS. CAROLINE COMPSON

Mrs. Compson's negligence and disregard contribute directly to the family's downfall. Constantly lost in a self-absorbed haze of hypochondria and self-pity, Mrs. Compson is absent as a mother figure to her children and has no sense of her children's needs. She even treats the mentally disabled Benjy cruelly and selfishly. Mrs. Compson foolishly lavishes all of her favor and attention upon Jason, the one child who is incapable of reciprocating her love. Mrs. Compson's self-absorption includes a neurotic insecurity over her Bascomb family name, the honor of which is undermined by her brother Maury's adulterous behavior. Caroline ultimately makes the decision to change her youngest son's name from Maury to Benjamin because of this insecurity about her family's reputation.

CANDACE COMPSON

Caddy is perhaps the most important figure in the novel, as she represents the object of obsession for all three of her brothers. As a child, Caddy is somewhat headstrong, but very loving and affectionate. She steps in as a mother figure for Quentin and Benjy in place of the self-absorbed Mrs. Compson. Caddy's muddying of her underwear in the stream as a young girl foreshadows her later promiscuity. It also presages and symbolizes the shame that her conduct brings on the Compson family.

Caddy does feel some degree of guilt about her promiscuity because she knows it upsets Benjy so much. On the other hand, she does not seem to understand Quentin's despair over her conduct. She rejects the Southern code that has defined her family's history and that preoccupies Quentin's mind. Unlike Quentin, who is unable to escape the tragic world of the Compson household, Caddy manages to get away. Though Caddy is disowned, we sense that this rejection enables her to escape an environment in which she does not really belong.

BENJY COMPSON

A moaning, speechless idiot, Benjy is utterly dependent upon Caddy, his only real source of affection. Benjy cannot understand any abstract concepts such as time, cause and effect, or right and wrong—he merely absorbs visual and auditory cues from the world around him. Despite his utter inability to understand or interpret the world, however, Benjy does have an acute sensitivity to order and chaos, and he can immediately sense the presence of anything bad, wrong, or out of place. He is able to sense Quentin's suicide thousands of miles away at Harvard, and senses Caddy's promiscuity and loss of virginity. In light of this ability, Benjy is one of the only characters who truly takes notice of the Compson family's progressing decline. However, his disability renders Benjy unable to formulate any response other than moaning and crying. Benjy's impotence—and the impotence of all the remaining Compson men—is symbolized and embodied by his castration during his teenage years.

QUENTIN COMPSON

The oldest of the Compson children, Quentin feels an inordinate burden of responsibility to live up to the family's past greatness and prestige. He is a very intelligent and sensitive young man, but is paralyzed by his obsession with Caddy and his preoccupation with a very traditional Southern code of conduct and morality. This Southern code defines order and chaos within Quentin's world, and causes him to idealize nebulous, abstract concepts such as honor, virtue, and feminine purity. His strict belief in this code causes Quentin profound despair when he learns of Caddy's promiscuity. Turning to Mr. Compson for guidance, Quentin feels even worse when he learns that his father does not care about the Southern code or the shame Caddy's conduct has brought on the family. When Quentin finds that his sister and father have disregarded the code that gives order and meaning to his life, he is driven to despondency and eventually suicide.

Quentin's Southern code also prevents him from being a man of action. The code preoccupies Quentin with blind devotion to abstract concepts that he is never able to act upon assertively or effectively. Quentin is full of vague ideas, such as the suicide pact with Caddy or the desire for revenge against Dalton Ames, but his ideas are always unspecific and inevitably end up either rejected by others or carried out ineffectively. Quentin's focus on ideas over deeds makes him a highly unreliable narrator, as it is often difficult to tell which of the actions he describes have actually occurred and which are mere fantasy.

JASON COMPSON IV

Jason's legacy, even from his earliest childhood, is one of malice and hatred. Jason remains distant from the other children. Like his brothers, Jason is fixated on Caddy, but his fixation is based on bitterness and a desire to get Caddy in trouble. Ironically, the loveless Jason is the only one of the Compson children who receives Mrs. Compson's affection. Jason has no capacity to accept, enjoy, or reciprocate this love, and eventually he manipulates it to steal money from Miss Quentin behind Mrs. Compson's back. Jason rejects not only familial love, but romantic love as well. He hates all women fervently and thus cannot date or marry and have children. Jason's only romantic satisfaction as an adult comes from a prostitute in Memphis.

Unlike Quentin, who is obsessed with the past, Jason thinks solely about the present and the immediate future. He constantly tries to twist circumstances in his favor, almost always at the expense of others. Jason is very clever and crafty, but never uses these talents in the spirit of kindness or generosity. Though he clearly desires personal gain, Jason has no higher goals or aspirations. He steals and hoards money in a strongbox, but not for any particular purpose other than selfishness. On the whole, Jason is extremely motivated but completely without ambition.

Jason's lack of achievement stems primarily from his relentless self-pity. Jason never forgives Caddy for the loss of the job at Herbert's bank, and he is unable to move past this setback to achieve anything worthwhile in his later life. Ironically, Jason becomes the head of the Compson household after his father's death—an indication of the low to which the once-great family has sunk.

MISS QUENTIN

Miss Quentin is the lone member of the newest generation of the Compson family. Many parallels arise between Miss Quentin and her mother, Caddy, but the two differ in important ways. Miss Quentin repeats Caddy's early sexual awakening and promiscuity, but, unlike Caddy, she does not feel guilty about her actions. Likewise, Miss Quentin grows up in a meaner, more confined world than Caddy does, and is constantly subject to Jason's domineering and cruelty. Not surprisingly, we see that Miss Quentin is not nearly as loving or compassionate as her mother. She is also more worldly and headstrong than Caddy. Yet Miss Quentin's eventual success in recovering her stolen money and escaping the family implies that her worldliness and lack of compunction—very modern values—indeed work to her benefit.

DILSEY

Dilsey is the only source of stability in the Compson household. She is the only character detached enough from the Compsons' downfall to witness both the beginning and the end of this final chapter of the family history. Interestingly, Dilsey lives her life based on the same set of fundamental values—family, faith, personal honor, and so on—upon which the Compsons' original greatness was built. However, Dilsey does not allow self-absorption to corrupt her values or spirit. She is very patient and selfless—she cooks, cleans, and takes care of the Compson children in Mrs. Compson's absence, while raising her own children and grandchildren at the same time. Dilsey seems to be the only person in the household truly concerned for the Compson children's welfare and character, and she treats all of the children with love and fairness, even Benjy. The last chapter's focus on Dilsey implies a hope for renewal after the tragedies that have occurred. We sense that Dilsey is the new torchbearer of the Compson legacy, and represents the only hope for resurrecting the values of the old South in a pure and uncorrupted form.

CHARACTER ANALYSIS

THEMES, MOTIFS & SYMBOLS

THEMES

Themes are the fundamental and often universal ideas explored in a literary work.

THE CORRUPTION OF SOUTHERN ARISTOCRATIC VALUES

The first half of the nineteenth century saw the rise of a number of prominent Southern families such as the Compsons. These aristocratic families espoused traditional Southern values. Men were expected to act like gentlemen, displaying courage, moral strength, perseverance, and chivalry in defense of the honor of their family name. Women were expected to be models of feminine purity, grace, and virginity until it came time for them to provide children to inherit the family legacy. Faith in God and profound concern for preserving the family reputation provided the grounding for these beliefs.

The Civil War and Reconstruction devastated many of these once-great Southern families economically, socially, and psychologically. Faulkner contends that in the process, the Compsons, and other similar Southern families, lost touch with the reality of the world around them and became lost in a haze of self-absorption. This self-absorption corrupted the core values these families once held dear and left the newer generations completely unequipped to deal with the realities of the modern world.

We see this corruption running rampant in the Compson family. Mr. Compson has a vague notion of family honor—something he passes on to Quentin—but is mired in his alcoholism and maintains a fatalistic belief that he cannot control the events that befall his family. Mrs. Compson is just as self-absorbed, wallowing in hypochondria and self-pity and remaining emotionally distant from her children. Quentin's obsession with old Southern morality renders him paralyzed and unable to move past his family's sins. Caddy tramples on the Southern notion of feminine purity and indulges in promiscuity, as does her daughter. Jason wastes his cleverness on self-pity and greed, striving constantly for personal gain but with no higher aspirations. Benjy commits no real sins, but the Compsons' decline is physically manifested through his retardation and his inability to differentiate between morality and immorality.

The Compsons' corruption of Southern values results in a household that is completely devoid of love, the force that once held the family together. Both parents are distant and ineffective. Caddy, the only child who shows an ability to love, is eventually disowned. Though Quentin loves Caddy, his love is neurotic, obsessive, and overprotective. None of the men experience any true romantic love, and are thus unable to marry and carry on the family name.

At the conclusion of the novel, Dilsey is the only loving member of the household, the only character who maintains her values without the corrupting influence of self-absorption. She thus comes to represent a hope for the renewal of traditional Southern values in an uncorrupted and positive form. The novel ends with Dilsey as the torchbearer for these values, and, as such, the only hope for the preservation of the Compson legacy. Faulkner implies that the problem is not necessarily the values of the old South, but the fact that these values were corrupted by families such as the Compsons and must be recaptured for any Southern greatness to return.

THEMES

RESURRECTION AND RENEWAL

Three of the novel's four sections take place on or around Easter, 1928. Faulkner's placement of the novel's climax on this weekend is significant, as the weekend is associated with Christ's crucifixion on Good Friday and resurrection on Easter Sunday. A number of symbolic events in the novel could be likened to the death of Christ: Quentin's death, Mr. Compson's death, Caddy's loss of virginity, or the decline of the Compson family in general.

Some critics have characterized Benjy as a Christ figure, as Benjy was born on Holy Saturday and is currently thirty-three, the same age as Christ at the crucifixion. Interpreting Benjy as a Christ figure has a variety of possible implications. Benjy may represent the impotence of Christ in the modern world and the need for a new Christ figure to emerge. Alternatively, Faulkner may be implying that the modern world has failed to recognize Christ in its own midst.

Though the Easter weekend is associated with death, it also brings the hope of renewal and resurrection. Though the Compson family has fallen, Dilsey represents a source of hope. Dilsey is herself somewhat of a Christ figure. A literal parallel to the suffering servant of the Bible, Dilsey has endured Christlike hardship throughout her long life of service to the disintegrating Compson family. She has constantly tolerated Mrs. Compson's self-pity, Jason's cruelty, and Benjy's frustrating incapacity. While the Compsons crumble around her, Dilsey emerges as the only character who has successfully resurrected the values that the Compsons have long abandoned—hard work, endurance, love of family, and religious faith.

The Failure of Language and Narrative

Faulkner himself admitted that he could never satisfactorily convey the story of *The Sound and the Fury* through any single narrative voice. His decision to use four different narrators highlights the subjectivity of each narrative and casts doubt on the ability of language to convey truth or meaning absolutely.

Benjy, Quentin, and Jason have vastly different views on the Compson tragedy, but no single perspective seems more valid than the others. As each new angle emerges, more details and questions arise. Even the final section, with its omniscient third-person narrator, does not tie up all of the novel's loose ends. In interviews, Faulkner lamented the imperfection of the final version of the novel, which he termed his "most splendid failure." Even with four narrators providing the depth of four different perspectives, Faulkner believed that his language and narrative still fell short.

MOTIFS

Motifs are recurring structures, contrasts, or literary devices that can help to develop and inform the text's major themes.

Time

Faulkner's treatment and representation of time in this novel was hailed as revolutionary. Faulkner suggests that time is not a constant or objectively understandable entity, and that humans can interact with it in a variety of ways. Benjy has no concept of time and cannot distinguish between past and present. His disability enables him to draw connections between the past and present that others might not see, and it allows him to escape the other Compsons' obsessions with the past greatness of their name. Quentin, in contrast, is trapped by time, unable and unwilling to move beyond his memories of the past. He attempts to escape time's grasp by breaking his watch, but its ticking continues to haunt him afterward, and he sees no solution but suicide. Unlike his brother Quentin, Jason has no use for the past. He focuses completely on the present and the immediate future. To Jason, time exists only for personal gain and cannot be wasted. Dilsey is perhaps the only character at peace with time. Unlike the Compsons, who try to escape time or manipulate it to their advantage, Dilsey understands that her life is a small sliver in the boundless range of time and history.

Order and Chaos

Each of the Compson brothers understands order and chaos in a different way. Benjy constructs order around the pattern of familiar memories in his mind and becomes upset when he experiences something that does not fit. Quentin relies on his idealized Southern code to provide order. Jason orders everything in his world based on potential personal gain, attempting to twist all circumstances to his own advantage. All three of these systems fail as the Compson family plunges into chaos. Only Dilsey has a strong sense of order. She maintains her values, endures the Compsons' tumultuous downfall, and is the only one left unbroken at the end.

Shadows

Seen primarily in Benjy's and Quentin's sections, shadows imply that the present state of the Compson family is merely a shadow of its past greatness. Shadows serve as a subtle reminder of the passage of time, as they slowly shift with the sun through the course of a day. Quentin is particularly sensitive to shadows, a suggestion of his acute awareness that the Compson name is merely a shadow of what it once was.

Symbols

Symbols are objects, characters, figures, or colors used to represent abstract ideas or concepts.

Water

Water symbolizes cleansing and purity throughout the novel, especially in relation to Caddy. Playing in the stream as a child, Caddy seems to epitomize purity and innocence. However, she muddies her underclothes, which foreshadows Caddy's later promiscuity. Benjy gets upset when he first smells Caddy wearing perfume. Still a virgin at this point, Caddy washes the perfume off, symbolically washing away her sin. Likewise, she washes her mouth out with soap after Benjy catches her on the swing with Charlie. Once Caddy loses her virginity, she knows that no amount of water or washing can cleanse her.

QUENTIN'S WATCH

Quentin's watch is a gift from his father, who hopes that it will alleviate Quentin's feeling that he must devote so much attention to watching time himself. Quentin is unable to escape his preoccupation with time, with or without the watch. Because the watch once belonged to Mr. Compson, it constantly reminds Quentin of the glorious heritage his family considers so important. The watch's incessant ticking symbolizes the constant inexorable passage of time. Quentin futilely attempts to escape time by breaking the watch, but it continues to tick even without its hands, haunting him even after he leaves the watch behind in his room.

MOTIFS

Summary & Analysis

April Seventh, 1928

Summary

Caddy smells like trees.   (See QUOTATIONS, p. 47)

NOTE: Benjy, the narrator of the difficult first section of the novel, has no concept of time. He portrays all events in the present—April Seventh, 1928— regardless of when they actually occurred in his life. The events that actually take place on April Seventh are rather insignificant. Far more important are the memories evoked by Benjy's experiences on that day. The summary below therefore includes not only the events that take place on April Seventh, but the past events that these cues from the present cause Benjy to recall.

On the day before Easter, 1928, a teenaged "Negro" boy named Luster is watching after Benjy, the severely retarded youngest son of the aristocratic Compson family of Jefferson, Mississippi. It is Benjy's thirty-third birthday, and Dilsey, the Compsons' cook and Luster's grandmother, has baked him a cake. Luster takes Benjy around the Compson property to search for a quarter he has lost. Luster had intended to use the quarter to buy a ticket to the minstrel show in Jefferson that weekend.

Luster leads Benjy to a nearby golf course, hoping to earn back his lost quarter by fetching lost golf balls from the rough. The golf course lies on a stretch of what used to be the Compson pasture, which Mr. Compson sold to developers to pay for his son Quentin's education at Harvard. When Benjy hears one of the golfers calling out to his caddie, he moans because the sound of the word "caddie" reminds him of his sister.

Luster helps Benjy climb through a fence. Benjy catches his clothes on a nail, which brings back a memory of a time when Caddy helped Benjy free himself from that same nail twenty-six

23

years before. This event occurred around Christmas, 1902, when Benjy was seven years old. In this memory, Mrs. Compson and her brother, Uncle Maury, are arguing inside the Compson house. Uncle Maury lives off of the Compsons' money and hospitality, and he is also having an affair with Mrs. Patterson, the Compsons' next-door neighbor. Uncle Maury uses young Benjy and Caddy as messengers to deliver his love letters to Mrs. Patterson. Mrs. Compson worries that Benjy will get sick from the cold, but she seems more concerned about the prospect of Benjy's sickness ruining her Christmas party than about his actual welfare. These memories of Caddy make Benjy moan again, which annoys Luster.

Returning to 1928, Benjy and Luster walk past the carriage house on the Compson property, which reminds Benjy of a time he saw the carriage house long ago during a trip to the family cemetery. In this memory, from approximately 1912 or 1913, Benjy and his mother are riding in the Compsons' carriage to visit the graveyard where Quentin and Mr. Compson were laid to rest. Dilsey mentions that Jason should buy the family a new carriage, as the current one is getting old. Jason mentions that Uncle Maury has been asking for money from Mrs. Compson. Luster chides Benjy for his crying once again.

Luster leads Benjy through the Compsons' barn. The barn swings Benjy's memory back to a time in 1902 when he and Caddy were delivering one of Uncle Maury's love letters to Mrs. Patterson. Benjy then thinks of a different time when he was delivering one of the letters by himself. In this memory, Mr. Patterson notices Benjy delivering the letter. Worried, Mrs. Patterson runs over, which scares Benjy. Mr. Patterson gets to Benjy first and intercepts the letter, learning of his wife's affair.

Back in the present, Benjy and Luster walk down toward the "branch," or stream, that runs through the Compson property. The branch causes Benjy to recall the day his grandmother, Damuddy, was buried in 1898. Benjy is only three years old at the time and his disability has not yet been discovered. In this memory, Quentin, Caddy, Jason, and Benjy are all playing together in the stream. The children's black attendant, Versh, tells Caddy she will be whipped for getting her dress wet, so she takes the dress off. However, Caddy gets mud on her underclothes. Walking back to the house, Caddy and Quentin worry that Jason will tattle to their parents about Caddy's wet clothes. The children see Roskus milking a cow in the barn, which shifts Benjy to a memory of Caddy's wedding in 1910.

SUMMARY & ANALYSIS

In this memory, Benjy and T.P., one of the Compsons' black servants, have gotten their hands on some champagne from the wedding, though T.P. thinks the beverage is merely "sassprilluh." The two boys are drunk and keep falling down as they watch some cows cross the yard. T.P. and Quentin get into a fight because T.P. has been teasing Quentin about Caddy. The fighting and the alcohol throw Benjy's world into chaos, and he begins to cry. Versh carries Benjy up the hill to the wedding party.

Benjy's memory of Versh carrying him returns his memory to 1898, when Versh was carrying Benjy up the hill after the Compson children played in the stream. In this memory, Versh tells the children that their parents have company over for dinner. When they reach the house, Jason tattles to Mr. Compson that Caddy and Quentin have splashed each other in the stream. Mr. Compson answers that the children will have to eat quietly in the kitchen because he has company over for dinner. Dilsey serves the children their meal, and as they eat, Benjy starts crying again. Quentin asks Dilsey if Mrs. Compson has been crying, and she deflects the question. Then, even Jason starts crying. Caddy teases Jason, knowing that he is upset because Damuddy is sick and he can no longer sleep in Damuddy's bed. The children walk down to Versh's house.

The memory of Versh's cabin reminds Benjy of several occurrences from 1910 and 1912. In 1910, Dilsey is singing in the kitchen, and Roskus complains that the Compsons are unlucky. In 1912, T.P. takes Benjy and little Miss Quentin—Caddy's illegitimate daughter—down to T.P.'s house, where Luster is playing in the dirt. Benjy steals Miss Quentin's toy, and when she gets upset, he cries. Roskus reiterates his conviction that the Compsons are unlucky. Dilsey and Roskus talk about the fact that Caddy's name is not to be mentioned around the house because of the disgrace her promiscuity has brought upon the family. Dilsey puts Benjy and Luster to bed.

We return briefly to the present, 1928. Luster has found a golf ball and Benjy wants to play with it. This returns Benjy to a series of memories about death. The first is from the evening in 1898 when the children had just finished dinner and walked down to Versh's house. Benjy wants to play with some lightning bugs T.P. has captured in a jar. Frony tells the Compson children that a funeral service is going on in the house. Damuddy has died and Mr. and Mrs. Compson have not yet told the children. Benjy recalls the death of the Compsons' horse, Nancy, and the buzzards that circled over the carcass afterward. He thinks briefly of Mr. Compson's death in

1912, then returns to the memory of Damuddy's death in 1898. The children worry that buzzards might pick at Damuddy's bones. Caddy is not convinced that a funeral is actually taking place, so she decides to spy on the adults through the parlor window. She climbs a tree and all three of her brothers catch a glimpse of her dirty underwear from below. When Benjy sees Caddy's soiled clothes he begins to cry again.

Benjy's memory briefly skips back to his drunken episode with T.P. at Caddy's wedding in 1910. He then thinks of a scene from 1905 when he became upset at the smell of Caddy's perfume. In this memory, Jason mocks Caddy for her "prissy dress" and claims that she is trying to act older than her age. Caddy washes off her perfume, but Benjy remains upset. Benjy thinks repeatedly that Caddy smells like trees. This returns him to the moment in 1898 when Caddy is up in the tree spying on the adults. In this memory, Dilsey reaches up, pulls Caddy down from the tree, and scolds the children for being outside past their bedtime.

Back in the present, Luster is still standing with Benjy as he plays in the stream. Luster tells Benjy not to approach the nearby swing because Miss Quentin is there with her boyfriend, the man with the red tie. This makes Benjy recall a time years ago when he saw Caddy and Charlie, her first suitor, kissing on the swing. In this memory, Benjy begins to cry very loudly when Caddy's suitor approaches. Charlie grows angry at Benjy's intrusion, which upsets Benjy even more. Caddy takes Benjy up to the house and cries, as she knows Benjy is upset with her for kissing Charlie. Caddy apologizes to Benjy and washes her mouth out with soap.

Benjy's consciousness then returns to the present day, 1928. He approaches the swing and interrupts Miss Quentin and the man with the red tie kissing on the swing. Miss Quentin gets upset with Luster for letting Benjy approach, and she runs back up to the house. Luster picks up an unused condom on the ground, thinking at first that it is his lost quarter. The man with the red tie asks where Luster found it. Luster replies that men come to visit Miss Quentin every night and that she always climbs down the tree outside her window to meet them outside. Benjy and Luster walk along a fence and come to a gate, where they see some schoolgirls walking by.

The gate and schoolgirls remind Benjy of a day in 1910, when he ran out of the house to look at some girls who were walking by the same gate. In this memory, Benjy manages to open the gate and run through it, scaring the girls. Wanting to tell the girls how much he misses Caddy, he catches up with one of them. The girl screams in terror. The scene ends as an unspecified assailant—presumably the father of one of the girls—attacks Benjy. That night, Mr. Compson is concerned and wants to know how Benjy got past the gate. He and Jason mull over the idea of having Benjy castrated as a precaution.

The narrative returns to the present. Luster tries to sell his golf ball to one of the golfers on the course, but the golfer takes the ball away from Luster. When the golfer calls for his caddie, Benjy starts moaning again because the word reminds him of Caddy. Luster gives Benjy a flower to try to calm him, and he tells Benjy that when Mrs. Compson dies, Jason is probably going to send Benjy off to an insane asylum in Jackson.

Luster and Benjy finally reach the Compson house. Dilsey yells at Luster, thinking Benjy is crying because Luster has been teasing him. Benjy sits down in front of the fire, which briefly reminds him of a time when he and Caddy sat near the fire just after his parents changed his name from Maury to Benjy. Back in the present, Dilsey lights the candles on Benjy's birthday cake, and Luster and Benjy eat some of the cake. Benjy reaches into the fire, burns his hand, and bursts into tears. Mrs. Compson enters the room, exasperated at her son's wailing. She goes on a tirade of self-pity, complaining that she is ill and cannot get any rest with Benjy making so much noise. Luster takes Benjy to the library to quiet him.

The library causes Benjy to remember another time he was in the library with Caddy. This was in 1900, when he was only five years old. In this memory, Caddy is trying to pick Benjy up to comfort him, but Mrs. Compson argues that Benjy is big enough to walk by himself. When Caddy attempts to comfort Benjy by letting him play with a cushion, Mrs. Compson complains that Caddy spoils Benjy too much. Jason and Caddy get into a fight because Caddy finds out that Jason has maliciously cut all of Benjy's paper dolls into pieces.

Returning to the present, Benjy continues to fuss while he and Luster sit in the library. Jason enters the room, clearly exasperated with Benjy. Luster asks Jason if he can borrow a quarter to go to the minstrel show, but Jason disdainfully refuses. Miss Quentin comes in and is still furious at Luster for allowing Benjy to sneak up on her when she was with the man with the red tie. Dilsey calls the family to supper. Benjy then recalls the evening in approximately 1909 when Caddy went on a date and lost her virginity. In this memory, Caddy comes home from the date, and Benjy cries loudly when he sees her.

She is ashamed and runs up to her room to avoid Benjy, which makes him very upset.

Back in the present, the family is seated at dinner. Miss Quentin complains that she does not like living in the Compson house. Jason rebukes her, and she threatens to run away. The argument between Jason and Miss Quentin escalates, and Dilsey tries unsuccessfully to mediate. Benjy's mind remains stuck in the past throughout this section, but the argument going on around him in the present keeps intruding. Miss Quentin curses Jason and storms off. Benjy runs off to an empty room and gets undressed. He and Luster see Miss Quentin sneak out of her bedroom window and run away.

Benjy's memory returns a final time to the night in 1898 when Damuddy died and Caddy soiled her underwear. In this memory, Dilsey is putting Benjy and the other Compson children to bed. Caddy's rear end is still muddy, but Dilsey does not have time to bathe her before bed. Caddy asks Mr. Compson if Mrs. Compson is sick, but he says she is not. Caddy holds Benjy as he falls asleep.

ANALYSIS

This first section of *The Sound and the Fury* is very difficult to navigate. Benjy, whose eyes are our only window on the Compsons thus far, is one of the most incomprehensible and challenging narrators in all of literature. Benjy's severe mental disability has left him with virtually no capacity for subjective thought. From his perspective, life is merely a string of images, sounds, and memories that he is unable to interpret, express, or organize in any meaningful way. Benjy does not understand any of the abstract concepts that underpin human existence, such as birth, death, love, family, virginity, intimacy, and marriage.

The greatest barrier to Benjy's ability to narrate is the fact that he has no concept of time. Benjy lives in an endless present tense. He interprets all events and memories as taking place in the present—April Seventh, 1928—regardless of when they actually occur in his life. Visual and auditory cues from the present cause Benjy to remember events from the past, but he does not understand that these remembrances are memories—he regards them just as if they were experiences from the present.

Faulkner uses Benjy's limitations to introduce one of the novel's key motifs, the human experience of time. Most humans rely on time to create a system of order out of the chaos of sensation, memory, and experience. For Benjy, however, time is a constant, not a flow, and is almost meaningless. The struggle we endure in reading Benjy's narrative forces us to confront what life would be like without the solidifying presence of time. Benjy offers us a few shattered pieces of truth, but they are difficult to discern.

Indeed, reading the chapter can be very disorienting. Benjy's flashbacks occur frequently and without warning, sometimes even mid-sentence. Faulkner sometimes marks these leaps in time with italicized text, but not always. The easiest way to tell when we are in the present is if we sense the presence of Luster: he plays a role only in the scenes from 1928. Compounding the temporal confusion of this section is the fact that several characters have the same names. Benjy's brother Quentin can easily be confused with Miss Quentin, Caddy's illegitimate daughter. Likewise, Benjy's brother Jason can be confused with the boys' father, Mr. Compson, who is also named Jason. Finally, we learn only implicitly that Benjy and Maury are the same person, as the Compsons renamed Benjy when they discovered his mental disability in 1900. The presence of Mrs. Compson's brother, Uncle Maury, confuses events in the novel even further.

One of Faulkner's primary reasons for using Benjy as the narrator of this first section is to hint at the tragic events and circumstances of the Compson family history through a completely objective voice that offers no commentary. Benjy's objectivity is based on his powerful, innate sense of order and chaos. He interprets the world by comparing his perceptions and experiences to the pattern of order and familiarity that exists in his mind. Benjy immediately notices if something—especially something involving Caddy—seems wrong or out of place. Any such deviation from Benjy's pattern of familiarity creates chaos in his mind and upsets him, making him cry or moan. Benjy's first whiff of Caddy's perfume, for instance, shocks his sense of order—he detects something awry and it disturbs him greatly.

Benjy's almost inhuman objectivity contrasts sharply with the perspectives of Quentin and Jason, who, as we will see in the next two sections, are both so skewed by their obsessions with Caddy that neither can narrate without significant embellishment or prejudice. Benjy's objectivity, on the other hand, allows us to gather clues on our own. His narrative gradually gives us an understanding of the relationships that govern the Compson household.

Mr. Compson is a distant figure, lost in his own cynicism and alcoholism. Likewise, Mrs. Compson is clearly ineffectual as a mother to her children, and her understanding of Benjy's needs is astonishingly feeble. She is constantly absorbed in self-pity and is neurotically insecure about her Bascomb family name. For whatever reason, Mrs. Compson favors Jason, the most wicked of her children. The only true role model and parent to the Compson children is Dilsey, who is the only real source of stability in the household. Though illiterate, Dilsey is faithful, devoted, and competent. She treats the children firmly but kindly, with clear concern for their welfare and character.

The Compson children's vastly differing personalities are apparent from a very young age. Caddy acts as a mother figure to Benjy and is his only real source of affection. However, Caddy seems somewhat headstrong, as we see when she insists that the other children "mind" her instead of minding Dilsey. Additionally, Caddy's muddying of her underwear in the stream as a young child foreshadows her later promiscuity. Caddy literally dirties herself, and the fact that Dilsey is unable to wipe the mud off suggests that Caddy's indiscretions will irreparably taint the family name.

Quentin is quiet and extremely close to and dependent upon Caddy. He is inordinately concerned with Caddy's welfare and neurotically protective of her. Jason, on the other hand, is distant from the other children. We see that he is cruel even as a young child, when he maliciously cuts up Benjy's paper dolls and tells on Caddy and Quentin for playing in the stream. Also, the fact that Jason constantly has his hands in his pockets hints at his future stinginess. Indeed, we see an example of this stinginess in Jason's refusal to lend Luster a quarter for the minstrel show.

The key events of the Compson family's history gradually begin to fall into place as well. We can construct a rough timeline of the events in Benjy's section based on a number of context clues embedded in the text. Since Benjy is turning thirty-three on April Seventh, 1928, he must have been born in 1895. In 1898, Damuddy died and Caddy got herself dirty in the stream. The Compsons changed Benjy's name from Maury to Benjamin in 1900. Benjy and Caddy got caught carrying the love letter from Uncle Maury to Mrs. Patterson in 1902. Caddy first used perfume in 1905, lost her virginity near the swing in approximately 1909, and was married in 1910. Quentin committed suicide at Harvard shortly thereafter. Benjy scared the neighborhood girls and was castrated in 1910, and Mr. Compson died of alcoholism in 1912.

These events reveal a pattern of moral decay within the Compson family. We see the first examples of this decay in Uncle Maury's affair with Mrs. Patterson and his use of the unwitting Caddy and Benjy as accomplices in his adultery. Uncle Maury is a member of the Bascomb family; his immorality is partly responsible for Mrs. Compson's obsession about her old family name and her decision to rename her son Benjamin. However, Mrs. Compson's symbolic attempts to distance herself from her brother's immorality are not effective, as we soon see Caddy exhibiting similar indiscretions.

The mud on Caddy's underwear prefigures her later promiscuity. We see that Caddy begins experimenting with boys at a young age, wearing perfume and having amorous encounters on the swing near the stream. Benjy senses that something is amiss or out of place, which disrupts the familiar patterns in his mind. He can sense Caddy's promiscuity, which in his mind is linked to the smell of her perfume. Indeed, Benjy becomes upset and cries every time he smells Caddy's perfume. The first time he smells the perfume, in 1905, Caddy washes it off. Still a virgin at this point, she is literally able to wash away the evidence of her indiscretions. However, when Caddy comes home from a date in 1909, Benjy cries loudly when he sees her. Caddy knows that she cannot simply wash away her sin as she could before. Aware that Benjy is upset, Caddy avoids him. This evasion makes Benjy cry even louder.

Some critics argue that the moment the three Compson boys look up into the tree and see Caddy's muddy underwear represents one of the climactic moments in the novel's theme of moral decay. Whether or not they know it at the time, all three boys are made aware of the curse on the Compson name at this moment. The promiscuity heralded by Caddy's dirty pants eventually unravels each brother's emotional or mental stability. Quentin commits suicide due to his despair over Caddy's lost purity. Jason lives a life of resentment and hatred after Caddy's promiscuity ruins his chances of getting the job that Caddy's husband had promised him. Caddy's banishment from the Compson household destroys the order in Benjy's world, leaving him confused, haunted, and longing futilely for her return.

The parallels we see between Caddy and her daughter, Miss Quentin, indicate that this moral decay in the Compson family will not end with Caddy's generation. Like Caddy, Miss Quentin discovers illicit sexuality on the swing near the stream. Additionally, just as he interrupted Caddy and Charlie kissing, Benjy interrupts Miss Quentin and the man with the red tie doing the same. It is notable, however, that Miss Quentin feels no guilt or need to wash away her sin as Caddy does. Because her mother has set a precedent of indiscretion, Miss Quentin does not feel that she has committed any wrong.

The events Benjy recalls reveal not only this pattern of moral decay within the Compson family, but also a pattern of death. Chronologically, the earliest past event that Benjy recalls is Damuddy's death. Damuddy never appears in the novel herself while alive. As a member of the older generation, she represents the old South of the nineteenth century, and her death can be seen as a marker of the end of that world. Importantly, the first event in the Compsons' spiral of tragedy is this symbolic death of the old generation. Benjy's castration can be seen as an extension of this specter of death to the next generation, as castration is a powerful symbol of the death of a family line.

Benjy also recalls the deaths and funerals of Mr. Compson, Quentin, and Roskus. The deaths are linked in his mind by the image of buzzards circling over the carcass of the Compsons' horse Nancy, and by the sound of the Compsons' black servants' ritual moaning over the dead. It is significant that Benjy recalls Roskus's death alongside Quentin's and Mr. Compson's, since this juxtaposition allows us to contrast Dilsey's suffering and mourning with the Compsons'. While the Compsons—especially Mrs. Compson—are shattered and unable to recover from the deaths in their family, Dilsey demonstrates considerable strength of spirit in her recovery from her husband's death. In this regard, Dilsey is the foundation of the hopes for resurrection and regeneration within the Compson family, which are hinted at later in the novel.

Ironically, the only people in the Compson household who seem aware of the family's decay and impending downfall are those who are least able to do anything in response: Benjy and the Compsons' black servants. Benjy's acute sense of order and chaos enables him to sense Damuddy's death, Caddy's promiscuity, Quentin's death, and other signals of the Compsons' decline. However, Benjy's disability prevents him from responding to these signals in any other way but moaning and wailing. Likewise, on the day of Mr. Compson's death, Roskus notes that the household is unlucky—"Taint no luck on this place." Though the black servants seem to have a sense for the Compsons' curse and anticipate the family's downfall, their position as servants makes it unlikely that their warnings will ever be heard or taken seriously.

JUNE SECOND, 1910

SUMMARY

If I'd just had a mother so I could say Mother Mother
(See QUOTATIONS, p. 48)

Quentin Compson wakes up in his dorm room at Harvard, hearing his watch ticking. He realizes that it is between seven and eight o'clock in the morning. Quentin remembers his father giving him the watch and saying that the watch might allow Quentin an occasional moment when he could forget about time. He thinks about the inevitability of his own awareness of time and remembers that St. Francis called death his "Little Sister," though, Quentin thinks, St. Francis never had a sister. Quentin gets up briefly, then goes back to bed. He has a memory of his sister Caddy's wedding announcement: *"Mr and Mrs Jason Richmond Compson announce the marriage of. . . ."* Caddy was married in April, just two months ago.

Quentin's roommate Shreve interrupts Quentin's thoughts, appearing in his doorway to remind him that the class bell will ring in only two minutes. Quentin says he had no idea it was so late, and that he will hurry to class. He tells Shreve not to wait for him. When Shreve leaves, Quentin goes to the window and watches the students rushing by. He spends a moment gazing at the unhurried Spoade, a Harvard senior who once mocked Quentin's virginity by calling Shreve his husband. He thinks about both his and Caddy's virginity.

Quentin suddenly remembers falsely confessing to his father that he had committed incest, and that he, not Dalton Ames, was the father of Caddy's child. He muses on Dalton Ames's name and remembers his father telling him that his great tragic feelings were meaningless and that there was no help to be had.

Quentin breaks the glass face of his watch against the corner of his dresser, cutting his finger in the process. The watch continues to tick. Quentin cleans up the glass and then packs a suitcase. He takes a bath and shaves. He puts the key to his trunk in an envelope along with two notes, which he addresses to his father. At the post office he mails the envelope, then tucks a similar note to Shreve inside his front pocket. Outside, Quentin looks for Deacon, a black man he knows, but when unable to find him he goes to a store for breakfast. Quentin then goes into a clock shop and shows his broken watch to the proprietor, but then tells the man not to fix it. Quentin asks if any of the clocks in the window are correct, but then asks not to be told what time it is.

Quentin buys a set of tailor's weights, hoping they will be "heavy enough," but he does not say for what. He goes to the train station and boards a train. As he rides, he remembers counting the seconds to himself as a child in school. He remembers that he never counted correctly, and never was able to guess exactly when the bell would ring. Quentin briefly remembers the day Benjy's name was changed from Maury. The train stops and Quentin gets off. He walks to a bridge and looks down at the water, thinking of shadows and of drowning.

Quentin sees Gerald Bland, a swaggering Harvard student, rowing across the river. Quentin goes through a series of painful memories, thinking of Caddy's promiscuity and her marriage to Herbert Head. He remembers his mother's letters about Caddy and Herbert, and Herbert's promise to give Jason a job in his bank. Quentin thinks vaguely about his mother's pride and emptiness, musing that Caddy never had a real mother and that he himself could never turn to his mother in times of need. Quentin finds Deacon, the black man he was seeking earlier. He gives Deacon the note he has written for Shreve, and asks him to take it to Shreve tomorrow.

Quentin rides a trolley, thinking abstractly about time and about his past. He remembers talking to Herbert Head two days before the wedding, and that he and Herbert nearly came to blows before Caddy came in and sent Herbert away. Quentin remembers telling Caddy she was sick and that if she was sick she could not be married. Caddy replied that because of her pregnancy she had "got to marry somebody." Quentin asked Caddy if she had slept with many men, and she answered vaguely. He then asked her whether she knew the identity of the father of her unborn child, and she again answered vaguely. Quentin then recalls another memory, when his father told him that the only reason Quentin was upset at Caddy's pregnancy was because he himself was still a virgin. Mr. Compson was relatively unconcerned with Caddy's pregnancy because he said that virginity was just a meaningless concept invented by men.

Quentin stands on a bridge looking down into the river. He remembers the time when he tried to persuade Caddy not to marry Herbert. Quentin told Caddy that Herbert was a "blackguard" who was thrown out of his club at Harvard for cheating at cards. He tried to convince Caddy to leave Jefferson with him, saying they could live off of the money meant for his Harvard tuition. Caddy refused, saying that Quentin's tuition money was raised through the sale of Benjy's favorite pasture, and that Quentin cannot drop out. Caddy is concerned that after their father's death Benjy will be put in the mental hospital in Jackson.

Quentin meets a little Italian girl in a bakery. He buys the girl some bread and she follows him. Quentin tries to find out where she lives. Finally, the girl's older brother Julio sees them and attacks Quentin, accusing him of kidnapping his sister. A constable arrives. As Quentin is being taken away to the squire, he sees Shreve, Spoade, Gerald Bland, and Mrs. Bland driving with some young girls. Quentin's friends accompany him to the squire's office. Quentin pays seven dollars in fines and is quickly released.

As they drive, Gerald Bland regales the group with stories about his exploits with women. Quentin remembers his confrontation with Caddy after discovering that she had had sex with Dalton Ames. Quentin frantically suggested to Caddy that they both kill themselves. Then he suggested that they claim it was Quentin who had taken Caddy's virginity and that they could go away together and even believe that it was true. Indifferently, almost numbly, Caddy accepted all of Quentin's suggestions. Afterward, in a frenzy, Quentin confronted Dalton Ames and threatened to kill him.

Quentin suddenly asks Gerald if he has a sister. Gerald says he does not, and Quentin hits him. Gerald fights back and gives Quentin a black eye. Quentin finds a trolley and rides back to Harvard. In his room, Quentin cleans a bloodstain off his vest and thinks about his mother. He remembers the time he told his father he had committed incest with Caddy, and that his father did not believe him. His father told Quentin that his feelings of despair about Caddy's behavior would quickly pass. The class bell rings outside. Quentin puts his watch in Shreve's desk, brushes his teeth, takes up his hat, and leaves the room.

SUMMARY & ANALYSIS

ANALYSIS
This section of the narrative relates Quentin's tormented and jumbled inner thoughts on the day that he commits suicide. Faulkner uses Quentin's narrative to continue his exploration of the human experience of time. Though not quite as disorienting as Benjy's narrative, Quentin's is nonetheless very abstract. Benjy is able to offer only vague impressions and objective observation. Quentin, however, has a conscious, subjective voice and frequently tends toward

abstract thought. Quentin's narrative plunges us into questions of human motivation, cause and effect, and circumstance that Benjy is unable to identify or consider.

Like Benjy, Quentin has memories of the past that intrude on his narrative constantly and without warning. Quentin's memory is complicated because it is largely intertwined with his fantasies. Sometimes it is difficult to tell which of his memories are based on events that actually occurred and which are based on fantasy or wishful thinking. Quentin's mind is far more complex than Benjy's, and, unlike Benjy, he is clearly aware that his flashbacks are just memories. Quentin, however, is just as likely as Benjy to associate past events with people or objects from the present.

Faulkner emphasizes the importance of time and memory in Quentin's world through the frequent appearance of clocks and watches. Quentin is effectively trapped in time, obsessed with his past and memories. He always notices the bells of the Harvard clock tower. The ticking of his watch haunts him even after he breaks the watch against his dresser. Quentin asks the owner of the clock shop whether any of the clocks is correct, but does not want to know what time it is. Additionally, Quentin repeatedly mentions walking into and out of shadows, which are constant reminders of time as gauged by the position of the sun throughout the course of a day. Unlike Benjy, who is oblivious to time, Quentin is so obsessed and haunted by it that he sees suicide as his only escape.

Clearly, the main thrust of Quentin's section is his struggle with Caddy's promiscuity. Quentin is horrified by Caddy's conduct, and he is obsessed by the stain it has left on the family's honor. Quentin, like Benjy, has a strong sense of order and chaos. However, while Benjy's order is based on patterns of experience in his mind, Quentin's order is based on a traditional, idealized Southern code of honor and conduct. This code is a legacy of the old South, a highly paternalistic society in which men were expected to act as gentlemen and women as ladies. Quentin believes very strongly in the ideals espoused under this traditional code: family honor; gentlemanly virtue, strength, and decency; and especially feminine purity, modesty, and virginity.

Caddy's promiscuity deeply hurts Quentin because he views it as dirty and shameful, a blatant violation of the ideal of femininity found in his Southern code. Quentin takes his code very seriously, as it forms the basis of order in his world. When Caddy's promiscuity breaks the code, Quentin attempts to maintain his sense of order by responding in a manner he considers honorable. Thinking that suicide is the only way to salvage the family name, Quentin tells Caddy that he will kill himself if she does the same. When she is uninterested, Quentin's next idea is to falsely accept the responsibility for fathering Caddy's child—a lie, but one he considers honorable and gentlemanly.

Quentin's anguish is compounded when he learns that his father really could not care less about Caddy's promiscuity. Mr. Compson is an articulate but cynical man. Recognizing the source of Quentin's torment, he discourages his son from taking himself so seriously. Mr. Compson argues that the concepts of virginity and purity—cornerstones of Quentin's paternalistic sense of Southern morality—are hogwash. Mr. Compson claims that virginity is a flimsy, unnatural idea that men have constructed. He believes that the concept is meaningless to women and should not be idealized. Quentin, on the other hand, finds his father's indifference completely dishonorable to the Compson name. Though Quentin never actually had sexual relations with his sister, he brings the story up again in front of his father. For Quentin, the false confession is a desperate attempt to assume Caddy's guilt and atone for it himself. However, Mr. Compson, like Caddy, dismisses Quentin's concerns. When Quentin sees that no one else in his family shares his code and his convictions, he reverts to suicide as the only remaining option, a means of exit while preserving his ordered universe.

Quentin's struggle to reconcile Caddy's actions with his own traditional Southern value system reflects Faulkner's broader concern with the clash between the old South and the modern world. Like a medieval code of chivalry, the old South's ideals are based on a society that has largely disappeared. Men and women like Quentin, who attempt to cling to these increasingly outdated Southern ideals, sense that their grasp is slipping and their sense of order disappearing. Their reliance on a set of outdated myths and ideals leaves them unequipped to deal with the realities of the modern world. Several characters in *The Sound and the Fury* embody this changing of the guard from old ideals to modern realities. Damuddy, the lone representative of the old South left in the Compson family, dies before any of the other action in the novel takes place. Miss Quentin, the lone member of the Compsons' new generation, is not only a bastard child, but has continued in Caddy's promiscuous ways without displaying any of the guilt Caddy feels about doing something wrong.

Quentin's obsession with his moral code is just one indication of his overall tendency toward thought rather than action. Quentin is clearly very bright, but his fixation on abstractions paralyzes him. He spends all his time thinking about nebulous concepts—time, honor, virginity, and so on—that have no physical presence. Existing only as words, these abstractions are difficult to act upon tangibly. Indeed, we see that Quentin is largely incapable of effective action: he frequently comes up with ideas, but never carries them out successfully. Quentin devises the double suicide pact with Caddy as a means of escape, but Caddy rejects the idea and escapes the Compson family without him. Likewise, Quentin talks frequently about confronting Dalton Ames and Gerald Bland, but his words win him nothing but two embarrassing beatings. The only actions we see Quentin take are meaningless and impotent, conforming to his Southern code but having no real outcome.

Though Quentin's moral code plays a large part in his anguish over Caddy's promiscuity, we get the sense that there is something more going on beneath the surface of this brother-sister relationship. When Quentin encounters the Italian girl in the bakery, he refers to her as a "little dirty child," which evokes a memory of Caddy. After Quentin's first encounter with a girl, Caddy disapproved of the girl and called her dirty. Just as Quentin seems jealous of the men Caddy encounters, we sense that Caddy is jealous not only of this first girl but of any girl Quentin might pursue. Faulkner implies that there is an unconscious sexual frustration between Quentin and Caddy, and that each of them might use his or her lovers to make the other jealous. Since Quentin is still a virgin, it seems likely that Caddy has made him far more jealous than he ever made her. While the shame of Caddy's promiscuity is clearly upsetting to Quentin, his despair may also contain elements of jealous rage.

APRIL SIXTH, 1928

SUMMARY

*I wouldn't lay my hand on her. The bitch that cost me
a job, the one chance I ever had to get ahead, that
killed my father and is shortening my mother's life
everyday and make my name a laughing stock in the
town. I wont do anything to her.*

(See QUOTATIONS, p. 49)

It is the morning of Good Friday, 1928, the day before Benjy's narration takes place. Jason Compson is in the Compson house, fighting with his mother and with his niece, Miss Quentin. Jason thinks
back on his family and his own personal history. His sister Caddy's
marriage to Herbert Head crumbled in 1911, when it became
apparent to Herbert that Caddy's unborn child was not his. Mrs.
Compson refused to take Caddy in, but Mr. Compson and Dilsey
saw to it that the family took in Caddy's child, Miss Quentin.
Jason assumed control of the household when Mr. Compson died
of alcoholism. Herbert Head had offered Jason a job at his bank,
but rescinded that offer when he divorced Caddy. This retraction
left Jason no choice but to work at the local farm-supply store.
Though Mrs. Compson hopes Jason will own the store one day,
Jason is bitter about having lost his bank job and having been
forced to work in the farm-supply store.

Now in his mid-thirties, Jason has grown into a devious and
mean-spirited man. He has concocted an elaborate scheme to
pocket the money Caddy sends him to support Miss Quentin's
upbringing. Mrs. Compson's poor eyesight and blind love for
Jason have prevented her from detecting his scheme. So far, Jason
has stolen nearly fifty thousand dollars from his sister and niece
over the course of fifteen years. He uses this extra money to
play the cotton market and to pay for a prostitute in Memphis.
Caddy is the only one who distrusts Jason and suspects that he
is scheming.

The seventeen-year-old Miss Quentin is a headstrong, rebellious,
and somewhat promiscuous girl who frequently skips school. Jason
constantly argues with Mrs. Compson and Miss Quentin over what
should be done with Miss Quentin and how she should be treated.
Jason threatens and insults Miss Quentin and nearly beats her with

his belt until Dilsey, as always, intervenes. Jason is finally forced to let Miss Quentin go, but makes a snarling promise that things are not yet settled between them.

Jason returns to his unfulfilling job at the farm-supply store and finds four letters, including one from Caddy and one from Uncle Maury. Jason recalls his father's funeral, after which he agreed to look after Miss Quentin as long as Caddy stayed away and continued to send money. The letter from Caddy contains a money order for Miss Quentin rather than the customary check. This turn of events throws a wrench in Jason's scheme, as Miss Quentin will have to sign the money order before it can be cashed. However, when Miss Quentin comes in to collect her money, Jason bullies her into thinking that the money order is for a mere ten dollars. He forces Miss Quentin to sign it without looking at the amount and sends her on her way.

Back at the Compson house for dinner, Jason barely tolerates his mother's self-pitying melodrama and the annoying sight of his idiot brother Benjy. Jason is deeply embarrassed about Benjy and wants to send him to the mental hospital in Jackson as soon as possible. After returning to work, Jason argues with his boss, Earl, about how long he can take for his dinner break. Earl accuses Jason of having stolen money from his mother to pay for his car. Several moments later, while Jason is in the back room tormenting Earl's black assistant, he sees Miss Quentin go by with a man wearing a red tie. Jason chases after them through the back alleys of Jefferson. He is interrupted by a boy with a telegram, who tells Jason that his account in the cotton market is significantly down.

Jason angrily goes home, and, driving back into town, is nearly run down by a Ford driven by the man with the red tie. Jason chases the Ford and looks for Miss Quentin and the man in some underbrush. He gets out, hoping to catch Miss Quentin red-handed with the man. Jason suddenly hears their car start and blow its horn. He runs back to his car and finds that Miss Quentin and the man have let the air out of one of his tires.

Jason makes it back to town, finishes his day at work, and returns home. Luster tells Jason that Miss Quentin and Mrs. Compson are upstairs fighting, and that Dilsey is trying to keep the peace. Luster wants to go to the minstrel show very badly and tells Jason he needs a quarter to buy a ticket. Jason has two tickets that he does not want, but he knows Luster does not have any money, so he burns up the two tickets in the stove while Luster watches.

Jason goes inside and Dilsey serves dinner. Jason does not explicitly mention that he saw Miss Quentin with the man in the red tie, but alludes to it indirectly several times. Miss Quentin angrily asks Mrs. Compson why Jason is always so hostile to her, and claims that she misbehaves because Jason has made her that way. Miss Quentin goes up to her room to study, but Jason suspects that she plans to sneak out of the house.

ANALYSIS

Faulkner sets the tone of Jason's section from the first sentence: "Once a bitch always a bitch, what I say." Jason has grown into a petty, sadistic, and bitter man, and we see that the form of his narrative reflects this hardened mind. Jason's narrative is clear, precise, swift, and almost completely emotionless. His clarity helps reveal several key plot details that the two previous sections have merely implied. Jason confirms that Benjy has been castrated, that Quentin drowned himself, and that Caddy was divorced. However, though a relief after the chaotic stream of consciousness of Benjy's and Quentin's narratives, Jason's section is ultimately disturbing in its clear depiction of the hatred and cruelty with which Jason runs the Compson family.

Though cunning and clever, Jason does not put his talents to good use. Instead, he succumbs to his own hatred and wallows in a sense of victimization. He resents Caddy for costing him the job at Herbert's bank, but fails to appreciate the fact that without Caddy he would never have been offered the job in the first place. The simple wickedness Jason displayed as child has intensified in his adulthood. He takes pleasure in tormenting everyone around him and takes strength from a conviction that, because he has been wronged, he is always right.

Considering that Jason is the new head of the Compson household, the family truly has sunk to an unfathomable low. Whereas his grandfather was a Civil War general and his great-grandfather the governor of Mississippi, Jason works as a clerk in a farm-supply store and steals from his own family. He is hardly of the same material as the ancestors who built up the family name. Ironically, however, Jason is the only one of the Compson children to win Mrs. Compson's love. Jason abuses his mother's trust, using it to blind her to the fact that he is stealing large sums of money from her. It is unclear why Mrs. Compson favors Jason so much, but perhaps it is because he shares Mrs. Compson's tendencies toward misery and self-pity much more than the other children.

Jason is not bothered by failing to live up to his ancestors' greatness because he is completely unconcerned with the past. Unlike Benjy and Quentin, Jason is wholly focused on the present and on manipulating the present for future personal gain. He does recall past events, but only concentrates on the effect those events have on him here and now. Jason dwells on Caddy's divorce, for example, only because it has left him in a menial and unfulfilling job. However, despite Jason's constant attempts to twist present circumstances to his own benefit, he does not really have any aspirations. He maintains overwhelming greed, selfishness, and focus on future gain, but does not use these to work toward any higher goal. Jason is all motivation with virtually no ambition.

APRIL EIGHTH, 1928

SUMMARY

> *Whoever God is, He would not permit that. I am a lady. You might not believe it from my offspring, but I am.* (See QUOTATIONS, p. 50)

It is Easter Sunday, 1928, the day after Benjy's narration and two days after Jason's. Dilsey walks up to the Compson house and manages to get the kitchen up and running despite the interference of Mrs. Compson and Luster. Luster tells Dilsey that Jason is angry because someone has broken the window in his room. Benjy eats his breakfast and whimpers. Jason emerges and testily sends Dilsey to call Miss Quentin to breakfast. There is no answer from Miss Quentin's room. Jason suddenly springs up the stairs, seizes his mother's keys, and unlocks Miss Quentin's door. The window is open and Miss Quentin is gone.

As Dilsey tries to comfort Mrs. Compson, Jason rushes to his strongbox and finds that it has been forced open. His papers are there, but all his money is gone. Jason calls the police and asks them to send a deputy to the house. He storms out. Meanwhile, Dilsey takes Luster, Frony, and Benjy to an Easter service at the local black church, where Reverend Shegog gives a boisterous sermon about the life and death of Christ. When they return to the house, they find that Jason still has not returned. Jason has gone to see the sheriff to demand help in tracking down Miss Quentin. However, the sheriff is suspicious of Jason's claim and sharply critical of the way he runs the Compson family. The sheriff refuses to help without more substantial evidence of Miss Quentin's wrongdoing.

Jason gasses up his car and goes to find Miss Quentin. On the way, Jason thinks about Lorraine, his mistress in Memphis. This thought reminds him of how angry he is to have been ripped off by a woman yet again. Jason drives to the town where the minstrel show is stopping next, since he believes that Miss Quentin's lover— the man with the red tie—works for the show. Jason rudely asks an old man where Miss Quentin and her lover are, but the old man takes offense and becomes violent, and Jason knocks him down. Jason tries to leave, but the old man comes after him with a hatchet. The man who runs the minstrel show rapidly leads Jason around the corner and convinces him that Miss Quentin and her lover are not there. Jason pays a black man to drive him back to Jefferson.

Back in town, Luster is driving Benjy in the carriage. As they arrive at the cemetery, Luster deviates from the usual course T.P. used to take, and Benjy begins howling at the unfamiliar route. Jason comes across Luster and Benjy. He hits Luster across the head, ordering him never to turn off the route Benjy is used to taking, and strikes Benjy in an attempt to quiet him. Benjy continues to howl. However, as Luster drives Benjy home, the familiar façades, doorways, windows, signs, and trees of the town of Jefferson all appear to Benjy in their ordered place, and he finally quiets.

> *I seed de beginnin, en now I sees de endin.*
> (See QUOTATIONS, p. 5 1)

ANALYSIS

The Sound and the Fury ends with the symbolic completion of the Compsons' downfall, but also hints at the possibility of resurrection or renewal. Importantly, this last chapter takes place on Easter Sunday, the day of Christ's resurrection and thus a powerful symbol of redemption and hope.

We may expect Caddy to narrate the last section, since she is in many ways the most important character in the novel, and the only one of the Compson children who has not had a chance to speak. However, Faulkner narrates this section himself, from a third-person perspective. This viewpoint takes us a step back from the

Compsons' inner world and provides a more panoramic view of the tragedy that has unfolded. The narrative voice Faulkner adopts is an objective one—similar to Benjy's in its ability to view the Compson world without resentment, but unlike Benjy's in that it is omniscient and relies on a more traditional mode of storytelling.

When Miss Quentin flees, the Compson name is definitively ruined. Caddy has been banished and neither of the remaining brothers is emotionally or mentally capable of passing the Compson name on to an heir. The storied, near-mythic past of the Compson family has disintegrated, with nothing remaining but a slobbering idiot and a bitter, wifeless, and now penniless farm-supply clerk. The Compsons are finished.

Miss Quentin's successful escape emphasizes the impotence and failure of the Compson men, especially in relation to the Compson women. Mr. Compson sets this precedent, constantly bowing to his wife's complaining and allowing her to pervert the family with her self-pitying and dependent nature. Likewise, we have seen that Benjy, Quentin, and Jason have all been dominated by Caddy in one way or another: Benjy cannot function without the sense of order Caddy provides him, Quentin cannot carry on with the knowledge of Caddy's promiscuity, and Jason cannot get past the fact that Caddy's out-of-wedlock pregnancy cost him a job. However, Caddy has never actively attempted to dominate her brothers. Each brother's impotence comes from an internal weakness or a form of self-absorption: Benjy's internal sense of order that relies entirely on Caddy, Quentin's neurotic ideal of feminine purity, and Jason's relentless self-pity. Caddy herself has never really *done* anything to harm her brothers directly.

Despite the Compsons' weakness and downfall, one source of hope and stability remains to hold the family together—Dilsey's simple, strong, protective presence. Dilsey adheres to the same traditional Southern values of religion and family upon which the original Compsons built their name. However, unlike the Compsons, Dilsey does not allow these values to be corrupted by self-absorption. When Dilsey arrives at the house to cook breakfast, she stays true to the task of setting the house in order despite constant interruption by the rest of the family. Unlike the rest of the family, she is not ashamed to bring Benjy to church with her. She loves Benjy as only Caddy has, and believes that God loves Benjy regardless of his lack of intelligence. Dilsey is not obsessed with the passage of time as Quentin is, and she is not overcome by the chaos of experience as the other Compsons are. Rather, she endures happiness and sadness with the same incorruptible will to carry on and sense of duty to protect those she loves. She looks on the Compson tragedy with sadness, but does not let it contaminate her own spirit. In her words, "I seed de beginning, en now I sees de ending."

Dilsey's words imply that the Compsons' downfall is part of a larger cycle. Indeed, Dilsey has, in effect, resurrected the original values of the Compsons' ancestors. The Compsons become carried away with the greatness of their own name, neglecting the strength of family in favor of self-absorption. Dilsey, on the other hand, is the antithesis of self-absorption. She maintains a strong spirit and a profound respect for an unpretentious, unadorned, yet powerful code of values. Dilsey is the redeemer of the Compson legacy, and provides an almost graceful landing after the resounding fall of the once-great household. In some respects, Dilsey's new role represents a reversal of the traditional Southern order: a black servant, once considered the lowest position in Southern society, is now the only torchbearer for the name of a prestigious white family.

The novel closes where it started, with Benjy. For a brief moment, we return to the world of order and chaos that exists in Benjy's mind. Benjy is almost unable to bear it when the carriage turns in an unexpected direction, as this deviation shatters his familiar, ordered routine. When Luster steers back onto the familiar route, Benjy becomes peaceful. Order prevails, and the elements of Benjy's experience return to the places where he expects to find them. Faulkner implies a hope that the Compson name itself, under Dilsey's guardianship, will likewise be set in order.

IMPORTANT QUOTATIONS EXPLAINED

1.   Caddy smells like trees.

Benjy remarks several times throughout his section that Caddy smells like trees or leaves. Caddy is Benjy's only mother figure and source of affection when he is young, and she provides the cornerstone of comfort and order in Benjy's mind. Benjy has relied heavily on his sister, and her absence plunges him into chaos. In his earliest memories of Caddy, Benjy pleasantly associates her youthful innocence with the smell of the trees in which they used to play. When Caddy becomes sexually active, Benjy notices the change she has undergone. The troubling realization corrupts his sense of order. Caddy knows Benjy is upset and begins to avoid him. Benjy laments this new distance between himself and his sister by saying that Caddy suddenly does *not* smell like trees. Trees are a pleasant memory associated with the affection and repose that Caddy has brought to Benjy's life, and when that order disappears, Benjy ceases to associate Caddy with that memory.

2. *If I'd just had a mother so I could say Mother Mother*

This quotation occurs several times toward the end of Quentin's section. Quentin is reflecting on how little affection his mother gave him as a child. Consumed by self-absorption and insecurities about her family name, Mrs. Compson showed affection for only one of her children, Jason. Quentin and Caddy formed a close bond as neglected, unloved outsiders, and Quentin developed an inordinately strong attachment to his sister. This bond leads to Quentin's despair over Caddy's promiscuity, which ends with his suicide. The object of Quentin's focus during the last hours of his life—his mother's absence and neglect—shows how significant and damaging Mrs. Compson's failure as a mother has been.

3.   I wouldn't lay my hand on her. The bitch that cost me
a job, the one chance I ever had to get ahead, that
killed my father and is shortening my mother's life
every day and made my name a laughing stock in the
town. I wont do anything to her.

In this quotation, in the final section of the novel, Jason explains to
the sheriff why he is chasing after Miss Quentin. Jason is character-
istically sarcastic and demonstrates the self-pitying notion that he is
a victim. He resents Caddy for divorcing Herbert Head and costing
Jason the bank job Herbert had promised. Jason has spent much of
his adult life in this way, resentful of others and cruel in return.
Jason is furious that Miss Quentin has escaped with his money, and
proceeds to blame her for all the family's misfortune. He is stung by
the knowledge that he has been dependent on Miss Quentin's presence as a source of stolen money. Jason knows that he will never
truly succeed because he never takes responsibility for his own fail-
ures. The irony here is that when Jason says he will not do anything
to Miss Quentin, his words are really true: she is now beyond his
grasp, which deepens his frustration.

4.   Whoever God is, He would not permit that. I'm a
     lady. You might not believe that from my offspring,
     but I am.

Mrs. Compson says these words in the final chapter, upon learning
that Miss Quentin has run away. She initially believes that Miss
Quentin might have killed herself, but she dismisses the thought,
believing that God would never allow her children to hurt her in
such a way. This comment provides a great deal of insight into Mrs.
Compson's thought process. First, it demonstrates the depth of her
self-absorption, as she implies that she interpreted her son Quentin's
suicide as an attempt to defy or hurt her. She still has no concept of
the depth of despair that Quentin experienced, and she arrogantly
assumes that his motivation for killing himself was merely to spite
her. Additionally, Mrs. Compson seems to think that her aristocratic social status gives her special privileges in the eyes of God.
Mrs. Compson displays this selfishness, obliviousness, and materi-
alism throughout the novel. She has discarded and corrupted the
values upon which her family was founded, yet still relies on ances-
try to justify her position in the world. Mrs. Compson is obsessed
with the concept of family—the greatness of her family history and
name—but she shows no capacity to love or care for her children,
the last hope she has for maintaining her legacy.

5.   I seed de beginnin, en now I sees de endin.

Dilsey says these words during the Easter church service in the final section of the novel, just after she learns that Miss Quentin has left. Dilsey's comment reveals her insight into the Compson family tragedy and her ability to see it in the context of a greater cycle. Dilsey has been present since the beginning, when the Compson children were only babies, and she is still here at the end, the culmination of the family's disintegration. In this sense, Dilsey represents a constant in the novel. She has maintained the pure Southern values of faith, love, and family that the Compsons have long abandoned. Dilsey endures the test of time, surviving because she has conviction and faith in her own vision of eternity that is completely free of worldliness or petty human concerns. Dilsey has no preoccupation with time because she has faith in a spiritual eternity, which enables her to see the tragedies of the Compson family with perspective and distance. Her acceptance of the passage of time makes her a calming and comforting presence. Dilsey accepts that she, like the Compson family, has a beginning and an end. She uses the time she is given to do as much good as she can, rather than wasting it on obsessions with the past.

QUOTATIONS

KEY FACTS

FULL TITLE
The Sound and the Fury

AUTHOR
William Faulkner

TYPE OF WORK
Novel

GENRE
Modernist novel

LANGUAGE
English

TIME AND PLACE WRITTEN
1928; Oxford, Mississippi

DATE OF FIRST PUBLICATION
1929

PUBLISHER
Jonathan Cape and Harrison Smith

NARRATOR
The story is told in four chapters by four different narrators: Benjy, the youngest Compson son; Quentin, the oldest son; Jason, the middle son; and Faulkner himself, acting as an omniscient, third-person narrator who focuses on Dilsey, the Compsons' servant.

POINT OF VIEW
Benjy, Quentin, and Jason narrate in the first person, as participants. They narrate in a stream of consciousness style, attentive to events going on around them in the present, but frequently returning to memories from the past. The final section is narrated in third-person omniscient.

TONE
The world outside the minds of the narrators slowly unravels through personal thoughts, memories, and observations. The tone differs in each chapter, depending on the narrator.

TENSE

Present and past

SETTING (TIME)

Three of the chapters are set during Easter weekend, 1928, while Quentin's section is set in June, 1910. However, the memories the narrators recall within these sections cover the period from 1898 to 1928.

SETTING (PLACE)

Jefferson, Mississippi, and Cambridge, Massachusetts (Harvard University)

PROTAGONIST

The four Compson children: Caddy, Quentin, Benjy, and Jason

MAJOR CONFLICT

The aristocratic Compson family's long fall from grace and struggle to maintain its distinguished legacy. This conflict is manifest in Caddy's promiscuity, her out-of-wedlock pregnancy, her short marriage, and the ensuing setbacks and deaths that her family members suffer.

RISING ACTION

Caddy's climbing of a tree with muddy drawers; Benjy's name change; Caddy's pregnancy and wedding; Quentin's suicide; Benjy's castration; Mr. Compson's death from alcoholism

CLIMAX

Miss Quentin's theft of Jason's money, and her elopement with the man with the red tie

FALLING ACTION

Dilsey's taking Benjy to Easter Sunday service and Benjy's trip to the cemetery

THEMES

The corruption of Southern aristocratic values; resurrection and renewal; the failure of language and narrative

MOTIFS

Time; order and chaos; shadows; objectivity and subjectivity

SYMBOLS

Water; Quentin's watch; Caddy's muddy underclothes; Caddy's perfume

FORESHADOWING

Caddy's muddy drawers when she climbs the pear tree foretell an inevitable dirtying of the Compson name that will never wash away.

Study Questions &
Essay Topics

Study Questions

1. *The opening section of* The Sound and the Fury *is considered one of the most challenging narratives in modern American literature. What makes this section so challenging?*

Benjy narrates the first section of the novel. Due to his severe mental retardation, he has no concept of time. This makes his narrative incoherent and frustrating at times because he cannot separate events in the past from those in the present. Benjy can only associate the images of his daily existence, such as the golf course and fence-post, with other occurrences of those images in the past. Benjy's fusion of past and present explains why he still haunts the front yard waiting for Caddy to come home from school—he does not understand that Caddy has grown up, moved away, and will never return.

Benjy's distorted perspective conveys Faulkner's idea that the past lives on to haunt the present. Benjy's condition allows Faulkner to introduce the Compsons' struggle to reconcile their present with a past they cannot escape. This unique narrative voice provides an unbiased introduction to Quentin's equally difficult section, in which Quentin struggles with his own distorted vision of a past that eventually overwhelms and destroys him.

2.   *Shortly after* The Sound and the Fury *was published, the
      noted critic Clifton Fadiman dismissed the novel, claiming
      that its themes were too "trivial" to deserve the elaborate
      craftsmanship Faulkner lavished on them. Many other
      critics have countered that the novel's themes extend
      beyond the story of the Compson family specifically, and
      grapple with issues central to human life in general. In
      what way might the themes of the novel extend beyond
      the story of the Compsons' decline?*

Although the plot of *The Sound and the Fury* is rather vague, the
novel demands a broader consideration of the history of the South
and the extended aftermath of the Civil War. The novel is set in the
first thirty years of the twentieth century, but many of the issues fac-
ing its characters involve old-fashioned, outdated traditions and
codes of conduct that are vestiges of the days before the Civil War.
To appreciate the novel's themes, we must view the events in the
Compson household as a microcosm of a succession of events
resulting, more or less, from the South's defeat in the Civil War. In
many of his novels, Faulkner focuses on this ultimate decline of the
Southern aristocracy since the Civil War. As the Compsons belong
to this aristocracy, *The Sound and the Fury* portrays their inevitable
demise. The members of the family—especially Mrs. Compson and
Quentin—fade away because they lead their lives according to outdated Southern aristocratic traditions that are incompatible with
the more modern, more integrated South of the early twentieth century. The Compsons are guilty of living in the past and, like many
Southern aristocratic families, they pay the ultimate price of seeing
their legacy gradually dissolved by the onset of modernity.

3.   *Faulkner has said that the character of Caddy was his
      "heart's darling"—her character inspired him to write the
      novel. Why is Caddy driven to pitfalls like promiscuity?
      What do you make of Mr. Compson's explanation that
      virginity is an ideal invented by men, which is utterly
      irrelevant to women?*

Caddy is at the center of most of the problems plaguing the Compson children. Quentin is obsessed with her. Jason is vindictive
toward her and jealous of her. Benjy is utterly reliant on her comforting presence. Indeed, despite her young age, Caddy serves as a
central force that holds the disparate members of the family
together. This loving, unifying presence becomes the root of Caddy's
and the Compsons' demise. When Caddy's husband discovers that
she is pregnant by another man, he divorces her, setting off a chain
of events that ultimately ruins the family. First, Jason loses the job
Caddy's husband had promised him. Jason resents Caddy so much
that he blames Caddy and her illegitimate daughter for all of his
own problems. His resentment builds into a hatred that haunts him
relentlessly, undermining every other opportunity that arises.

   Quentin's obsession with Caddy drives him to suicide after she
loses her virginity. Mr. Compson foresees the danger in Quentin's
obsession long before it pushes his son to suicide. He tries to calm
Quentin by explaining that virginity is just a tradition and code of
the old South, and that it ultimately only matters to men who take
those traditions and codes too seriously. In a sense, Mr. Compson's
insight provides a refreshing alternative to the strict adherence to
past traditions that the rest of the Compson family follows. Any
hope, however, that Mr. Compson's advice might lead to a turn-
around in his son's obsession vanishes with Quentin's suicide, which
devastates Mr. Compson and likely contributes to his death from
alcoholism not long thereafter. The cold, selfish, compassionless
Jason IV rises up to run the family, which eventually leads to the
Compsons' demise.

SUGGESTED ESSAY TOPICS

1.   One of the most wrenching sections of the novel is Quentin's confrontation with Caddy following the loss of her virginity. What drives Quentin to propose mutual suicide and to conceive of the idea of incest as a solution to their problems? Even in the absence of sex between them, is there something incestuous about Quentin and Caddy's relationship?

2.   Compare and contrast the three major narrators of the novel: Benjy, Quentin, and Jason. How are their sections alike? How do they differ? What are the consequences of Faulkner's decision not to introduce an easily readable chapter until the second half of the novel?

3.   Think about Benjy's character. What purpose, if any, does he serve beyond the novel's opening section? Is he a believable character?

4.   Perhaps the single most important theme in *The Sound and the Fury* is the presence of time in human life. How is that relationship explored throughout the four sections of the novel?

5.   Why do you think the fourth section of *The Sound and the Fury,* the section focusing on Dilsey, is so technically different than the other three? For example, why would Faulkner write this section in the third person while the others are all written in the first person?

QUESTIONS & ESSAYS

Review & Resources

Quiz

1. Which of the Compson children is the eldest?

   A. Benjy
   B. Caddy
   C. Jason
   D. Quentin

2. Dilsey is the Compsons':

   A. Cook
   B. Neighbor
   C. Cat
   D. Milkman

3. What plaything of Benjy's does Jason destroy?

   A. His rocking horse
   B. His rubber ball
   C. His paper dolls
   D. His crayons

4. Faulkner's fictional locales of Yoknapatawpha County and Jefferson are supposedly in which state?

   A. Louisiana
   B. Mississippi
   C. Alabama
   D. Georgia

5. How does Luster hope to earn back the money he has lost?

   A. Mow lawns
   B. Search for lost golf balls
   C. Open a lemonade stand
   D. Work in Jason's store

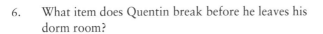

6. What item does Quentin break before he leaves his dorm room?

   A. His glasses
   B. His gold chain
   C. His mirror
   D. His watch

7. As children, what do Caddy and Benjy frequently deliver to the Pattersons' house?

   A. Cookies and desserts from their kitchen
   B. Business papers of Mr. Compson's
   C. Fresh milk from their cows
   D. Love letters from Uncle Maury to Mrs. Patterson

8. Which piece of Caddy's clothing gets muddy when she is playing in the stream?

   A. Her underwear
   B. Her blouse
   C. Her shoes
   D. Her dress

9. What does Luster plan to do with his money before he loses it?

   A. Spend it at the toy store
   B. Attend a minstrel show in town
   C. Repay his mother for money he had borrowed
   D. Pay for a bet he had lost

10. Where does Quentin encounter the little Italian girl?

    A. A post office
    B. A bakery
    C. A bookstore
    D. A clock repair shop

11.   What does Quentin suggest Caddy and he do?

  A.   Kill themselves
  B.   Move away and live off of Quentin's tuition money
  C.   Concoct a false story about the father of Caddy's child
  D.   All of the above

12.   What was Faulkner's source for the title of *The Sound and the Fury?*

  A.   The Bible
  B.   Milton's *Paradise Lost*
  C.   Shakespeare's *Macbeth*
  D.   Gibbon's *The Decline and Fall of the Roman Empire*

13.   How does Quentin commit suicide?

  A.   He drowns himself
  B.   He shoots himself
  C.   He hangs himself
  D.   He drinks himself to death

14.   Where does Jason work?

  A.   The local grocery store
  B.   The local bank
  C.   The local farm-supply store
  D.   The local bookstore

15.   What color is the tie that Miss Quentin's suitor is wearing when Jason sees him?

  A.   Blue
  B.   Green
  C.   Red
  D.   Black

16.   What does Jason do with his two tickets to the minstrel show?

  A.   He burns them
  B.   He loses them
  C.   He gives them to Luster
  D.   He sells them to Luster

17. Why does Benjy get upset on the way to the cemetery?

    A. He hears a golfer call to his caddie, which reminds him of Caddy

    B. Luster deviates from the normal route back to the house

    C. He smells trees alongside the road and thinks of Caddy

    D. Jason is mean to him

18. The novel's climactic events in 1928 take place on what Christian holiday?

    A. Easter

    B. Christmas

    C. All Saints' Day

    D. Ash Wednesday

19. Mrs. Compson has poor:

    A. Hearing

    B. Vision

    C. Posture

    D. Hygiene

20. Jason uses the money he steals from Caddy to invest in the market for what commodity?

    A. Gold

    B. Oil

    C. Soybeans

    D. Cotton

21. Miss Quentin steals Jason's:

    A. Car

    B. Money

    C. Business papers

    D. Gold watch

REVIEW & RESOURCES

22. Benjy undergoes which operation?

    A. Castration
    B. Tonsillectomy
    C. Appendectomy
    D. Lobotomy

23. How does the sheriff react to Jason's story about Miss Quentin's theft?

    A. He is doubtful and refuses to help without proof
    B. He immediately chases after Miss Quentin
    C. He goes to the Compsons' house to check on Mrs. Compson
    D. He is too busy to take the case so he assigns it to his deputy

24. At Caddy's wedding, the beverage T.P. thinks is "sassprilluh" is really what?

    A. Whiskey and soda
    B. Root beer
    C. Champagne
    D. Tonic water

25. One of Faulkner's major themes is the decline of Southern

    A. Cooking
    B. Aristocratic families
    C. Fashion sense
    D. Culture and fine arts

ANSWER KEY:

1: D; 2: A; 3: C; 4: B; 5: B; 6: D; 7: D; 8: A; 9: B; 10: B; 11: D; 12: C; 13: A; 14: C; 15: C; 16: A; 17: B; 18: A; 19: B; 20: D; 21: B; 22: A; 23: A; 24: A; 25: B

SUGGESTIONS FOR FURTHER READING

BLEIKASTEN, ANDRE. *The Most Splendid Failure: Faulkner's* THE SOUND AND THE FURY. Bloomington, Indiana: Indiana University Press, 1976.

BLOOM, HAROLD, ed. *Modern Critical Interpretations: William Faulkner's* THE SOUND AND THE FURY. New York: Chelsea House, 1988.

COWAN, MICHAEL H., ed. *Twentieth Century Interpretations of* THE SOUND AND THE FURY. Englewood Cliffs, New Jersey: Prentice, 1968.

IRWIN, JOHN T. *Doubling and Incest / Repetition and Revenge: A Speculative Reading of Faulkner.* Expanded edition. Baltimore: Johns Hopkins University Press, 1996.

KINNEY, ARTHUR F. *Critical Essays on William Faulkner: The Compson Family.* Boston: G.K. Hall, 1982.

MINTER, DAVID. "Faulkner, Childhood, and the Making of *The Sound and the Fury." American Literature* 51 (1979): 376–93.

POLK, NOEL, ed. *The American Novel: New Essays on* THE SOUND AND THE FURY. Cambridge: Cambridge University Press, 1993.

WEINSTEIN, PHILIP, ed. *William Faulkner's* THE SOUND AND THE FURY: *A Critical Casebook.* New York: Garland, 1982.

REVIEW & RESOURCES

SparkNotes Study Guides: